Louis Marie de Montfort

His Life, Message and Teaching

by
Paul R. Allerton, SMM

*All booklets are published thanks to the
generous support of the members of the
Catholic Truth Society*

CATHOLIC TRUTH SOCIETY
PUBLISHERS TO THE HOLY SEE

Contents

Preface 3

Early Life 5

Training for the Priesthood 14

Early Hopes and Frustrations 19

Missions in the Diocese of Nantes 28

Last Years 38

The Legacy of a Saint 50

Images: Pages 6, 10, 21, 27 and 47 courtesy of the author, the Montfort Missionaries and the Daughters of Wisdom. Page 35 © The Calvary of Pontchâteau, © Roger Hollingsworth. Page 51 every effort has been made to trace the copyright holders. The publisher would be grateful to receive any further information.

All rights reserved. First published 2016 by The Incorporated Catholic Truth Society, 40-46 Harleyford Road London SE11 5AY Tel: 020 7640 0042 Fax: 020 7640 0046. © 2016 Paul R. Allerton, SMM.

ISBN 978 1 78469 094 6

Preface

The year 2016 sees the three hundredth anniversary of the death of St Louis Marie Grignion de Montfort (1673-1716), one of the greatest teachers of devotion to the Blessed Virgin that the world has seen. His teaching has inspired so many people, including Pope St John Paul II, St Maximilian Kolbe, Frank Duff (founder of the Legion of Mary), the late Cardinal Léon-Joseph Suenens, Venerable Mother Mary Potter (foundress of the Little Company of Mary), Fr Frederick William Faber, Cardinal Herbert Vaughan (founder of the Mill Hill Missionaries) and a host of others. But he was not only a teacher of Marian devotion; he was a missionary preacher who, by his inspired preaching and holy life, brought renewal to vast areas of north-west France in his own short lifetime, a ministry which has been continued all over the world for three hundred years by his followers, particularly in the three religious institutes that owe their beginnings and their inspiration to him: the Company of Mary (Montfort Missionaries); the Daughters of Wisdom (Sisters of La Sagesse) and the Brothers of St Gabriel.

It seems opportune to present this great saint and missionary once again to the English-speaking Catholic

Church, especially in the British Isles, as we remember the salient events of his life and the legacy he left to the whole Church. There have already been a number of biographies of the saint in English, including the slightly revised and re-issued *The Man Called Montfort*, by Fr Edward Bolger, SMM,[1] first published at the time of his canonisation by Pope Pius XII in 1947 - a deservedly popular life written in a lively style. Others are now, unfortunately, out of print. This little book cannot hope to supply the need for a new critical biography, but its author hopes that it will remind the Catholic people of such a great saint in the tercentenary year of his death.

---

[1]Published by Montfort Press, Liverpool, *http://montfortpress.montfort. org.uk*

Early Life

Louis Grignion was born on 31st January 1673 in the little town of Montfort-sur-Meu (then known as Montfort-la-Cane), approximately 30 km to the west of Rennes, the provincial capital of Brittany. His father, Jean-Baptiste Grignion, was a somewhat impecunious 'procureur' (a sort of solicitor) in the court in Montfort; he had ambitions to rise higher in the social scale, and he owned some agricultural properties in the region of Montfort, but lacked the financial resources and the business acumen to achieve his ambitions. Louis's mother, Jeanne Robert, was the daughter of a municipal magistrate in Rennes, and had three brothers who were priests. Louis was not the first child born to the couple; a brother born in 1672 had died at the age of five months, making Louis the eldest surviving child in a family that numbered in all eighteen children, though seven of these died in infancy or early childhood (not unusual in those days), while another died at the age of eight or thereabouts. Of those ten who survived into adulthood (four males, six females), three of the boys became priests (two diocesan priests and one a Dominican Friar), while two of the girls became nuns. These latter figures certainly argue for a good Christian

Birthplace of Louis Marie in Montfort-sur-Meu.

upbringing, which raises some doubts about the accuracy of the picture sometimes painted of their father as being a man of violent temper and over-concerned with wealth. Two more of the girls married and had children, while only one of the boys raised a family of his own. To have borne eighteen children in little more than nineteen years must certainly have placed a great strain on Jeanne, the mother, and, being apparently of a quiet and gentle nature, her life cannot have been easy. This may well be why Louis seems to have had a closer relationship with her than with his father, even in his adolescent years, when a boy will normally be gravitating more to his father.

Baptism

Louis was baptised, as the custom then was, the day after his birth, in the parish church of Saint-Jean, one of three parishes in the town of Montfort in those days. The only name given to him at his Baptism was Louis, though today he is better known as Louis Marie. It is likely that he took the name Marie, in honour of his beloved spiritual Mother, the Blessed Virgin Mary, at his Confirmation, though we have no certainty regarding this. Probably just a few days after his birth, he was put out to a wet-nurse (again a common custom among bourgeois families in France at the time). Tradition says that his wet-nurse was the wife of one of his father's tenants on a small-holding in the hamlet of La Bachelleraie, a mile or so outside Montfort; her name has come down to us as 'Mère André', André having been her maiden name. Some two years later, the whole Grignion family moved from Montfort to a 'manor-house' (in reality a farm) called 'Le Bois Marquer' near the town of Iffendic, a few miles from Montfort. Louis would certainly not have come home from his wet-nurse by that time, and perhaps not for one or two years more; so that he actually spent very little time living in Montfort itself. Yet later in his life he adopted the name 'Montfort' in preference to his family name of Grignion, signing himself most often as 'Louis Marie de Montfort', and being universally known as 'Father de Montfort'. Why?

It would appear that it was because he saw the moment of Christian Baptism as the most significant moment in a person's life, including his own. In all his missionary work as a priest as well as in his writings, the renewal of baptismal commitment was a privileged theme. For himself, Montfort was the place of his Baptism, his entry into the real life of relationship with God, so Montfort remained for him a very important place.

It has been conjectured that Louis spent as many as five or six years with his wet-nurse at La Bachelleraie - perhaps the most formative years of a child's life. In later life he showed a distinct preference for the ordinary, simple people, the sort among whom he lived in La Bachelleraie, as opposed to the bourgeois, middle-class people represented by his own family. Perhaps it was here that he developed this preference, which was sometimes seen by those who opposed him as a rather insulting rejection of the bourgeoisie.

Education

We have little information regarding Louis's early education. Perhaps he was given lessons by the parish priest of his new parish of Iffendic. He would certainly have absorbed lessons in the love of God from his own mother, perhaps aided by the magnificent stained-glass window in the east end of the church in Iffendic which portrays scenes from the life of St Peter, the parish patron, in vivid colours. We are told by his earliest biographers (who either had known him personally or who had solicited information concerning him from those who had known him, including his maternal uncle, the Abbé Allain Robert), that he showed signs of an unusual piety from a very early age. Even accepting that there was a somewhat exaggerated desire to exalt his sanctity that was common in hagiographies of that time, it does seem that even then he was someone who seemed destined to become renowned for an unusual holiness of life.

In 1684, when he was eleven years old, Louis was sent to the Jesuit College of St Thomas Becket in Rennes, which he attended for the next eight or nine years, moving from the usual secondary education provided there into the study of philosophy and theology that was also provided for those destined for the priesthood. Apart from the excellent classical education provided by the Jesuits, echoes of which we can see in the clarity of Louis's later writing as well as in the rigorous thought that is evident in all that he wrote, other things seem to have influenced him from his time at the Jesuit College. On the pedagogical level, the College's use of theatre - a common element in all Jesuit education of the time - seems to have given him inspiration for the use of theatrical devices in the missions he was to give in later life. We can see echoes of this in some of the more than 160 hymns that he wrote for use in his missions.

Statue of Our Lady of Wisdom said to be carved by Louis Marie at Saint-Lazare 1707-08, now kept in his birthplace in Montfort-sur-Meu.

Devotion to the Blessed Virgin

A more significant influence from this time at the Jesuit
College was the strong emphasis placed by the Jesuits on
devotion to the Blessed Virgin. All Jesuit Colleges of the
day had their 'Congregations' dedicated to the Blessed
Virgin, in which the more pious students could be enrolled,
and which nourished a solid understanding of the role of
Mary in the life of the Christian. Louis Grignion was duly
enrolled in the Congregation of the Blessed Virgin at St
Thomas's, and we are told that he showed himself one of the
most fervent of the 'congréganistes'. Even as a child he is
said to have had a strong devotion to his 'good Mother' - his
fellow-student, Jean-Baptiste Blain, who would later write
a brief life of St Louis Marie, says that "love of Mary was
almost as if innate in M Grignion" - , and the Jesuit teaching
and example only strengthened this. His growing awareness
of Mary's place is reflected in the numerous visits he used
to make at this time to various shrines of Our Lady to be
found in the town of Rennes. Later, he would teach, both
in his writings and in his preaching, that devotion to Mary
is one of the most important means of being in the right
relationship with Jesus himself; and here in Rennes, we can
see the foundations of his teaching being solidly laid.

Not only his strong devotion to Mary, but also his intense
interest in parish missions, and his deep love of and care
for the poor, were nourished during this period in Rennes.
The one who seems to have exercised most influence on

him in these two areas was a young diocesan priest, the Abbé Julien Bellier. He himself had for a number of years worked occasionally in the giving of parish missions by a team headed by M Jean Leuduger, a priest of the Diocese of Saint-Brieuc, who was one of the foremost proponents of parish missions at that time. Abbé Bellier used to gather a group of spiritually fervent students of the Jesuit College, including young Louis, every week, to talk with them and encourage their spiritual efforts. He would often speak of the work of M Leuduger and the parish missions, and he seems to have fired the imagination of Louis Grignion in this regard. He was also a determining influence in Louis's care for the poor, as he used to send some of his young friends off, two by two, after his spiritual conferences, to visit the poor in the General Hospital of Saint-Yves in Rennes. We know that Louis learnt his lesson well from a number of stories told of him during those student days. For example, he took it into his own hands to help a rather impoverished fellow-student to obtain a much-needed suit of decent clothes, by begging among his fellow-students and, when he still had not been able to amass enough to pay for it, going to the tailor and telling him: "I have done what I can; now it is up to you to supply the rest!" Perhaps surprisingly, the tailor complied with this request. This incident is a foretaste of Louis's regular way of acting later in his life, when he would combine practical actions with a deep trust in Providence.

Vocation

It seems that Louis Marie had finished his course in philosophy and had already begun the study of theology, having felt called to become a priest, when he was given the opportunity to continue his theological studies at the famous Seminary of Saint-Sulpice in Paris. A visitor to his father's house, a certain Mlle de Montigny, not only spoke glowingly of this seminary, but offered to obtain sufficient funds to enable Louis Marie to gain a place there. Accordingly, Louis Marie set off for Paris about the beginning of November 1692 or 1693.

Training for the Priesthood

After bidding farewell to his family, some of whom accompanied him as far as the Cesson bridge just to the east of Rennes, Louis Marie, with a gesture typical of what would become normal for him, embarked on a new life, in which he was determined to depend entirely on divine Providence for all his needs, and give himself completely to the service of God. He had been offered a horse to take him at least some of the 300 km or so to Paris, and had been given a new suit of clothes and a certain amount of money (not very much) to start his new life. He refused the horse, preferring to travel (as he would for the rest of his life) on foot, despite the onset of winter. And we are told that, no sooner was he out of sight of his family than he gave away all the money he had to poor people along the way, and even exchanged his new suit of clothes for the rags of a beggar. This was no meaningless or adolescent gesture; from now on, he really would lead a life of poverty and abandonment to Providence.

Arrival in Paris

He arrived in Paris, after a wet and miserable journey, only to find that the money provided by Mlle de Montigny was not nearly sufficient to gain him a place in the great

Saint-Sulpice Seminary, nor even in what was known as the 'Little Saint-Sulpice' - an annexe reserved for those of more slender means. Instead he found a place in a community established nearby by a kindly priest, Fr de la Barmondière, for poor students studying for the priesthood. But even there, his future was precarious, as the funds provided for him dried up, and it was only through the ingenuity of Fr de la Barmondière finding him a means of earning himself a little money by watching over recently-deceased people that he could stay on. He had been in Paris for barely two years when Fr de la Barmondière died, and he then found himself in another small community of poverty-stricken clerical students run by a certain Fr Boucher. Living conditions here were worse than in the previous community, and after about a year Louis Marie was taken seriously ill, and had to be admitted to the 'Hôtel-Dieu', the hospital for the poor close by Notre-Dame in the city. The poor conditions in Fr Boucher's establishment may have been one of the main causes of his illness, but his own severe asceticism, for which he was already known, cannot have helped. It was feared by all that he would die, but somehow he recovered, and when he was finally released from the hospital he found that he had been offered a place in the 'Little Saint-Sulpice'. It seems that his reputation for holiness was beginning to be appreciated, and it is said that a 'Te Deum' was sung in thanksgiving when he entered the seminary.

Life at Saint-Sulpice Seminary

Saint-Sulpice Seminary had been founded by Jean-Jacques Olier about 1641 to respond to the call made by the Council of Trent in the previous century for a much-improved training for priests in the Catholic Church. It was, at the time of St Louis Marie, considered to be one of the finest seminaries in France, indeed in the whole of Europe. Its academic programme was affiliated with the University of the Sorbonne, and so was highly considered, while its formation in Christian and priestly spirituality was unrivalled. Louis Marie had a somewhat strange relationship with this establishment and its directors. Despite their respect for this young man as, in many ways, a model of Christian virtue, some of them were very suspicious of his motives for the asceticism that he practised, evidently thinking that he might just be showing off. So they did all they could to test him, for a time making his life, humanly speaking, a misery. Despite the fact that he came through this trial with flying colours, it being acknowledged by most of his Superiors that his piety was genuine, some suspicion of his motives remained, it seems, and relations between him and the seminary staff was always somewhat ambiguous, as will be seen some years later.

Part of the problem was the image of the priest that was fostered by the whole culture of Saint-Sulpice: that of an eminently respectable leader, who would never stand out as 'singular' or eccentric in any way, but would be an example of level-headedness and moderation in all things. Many of the alumni of Saint-Sulpice Seminary would make a good career for themselves in the Church. The trouble was that Louis Marie Grignion could never fit into this mould; he was not in the least concerned with making a career for himself, and his enthusiastic embracing of both devotion to the Blessed Virgin and the practice of penance was seen, both by many of the staff of the seminary as well as by most of the students, to be 'over-the-top'. He was already gaining the reputation for 'singularity' or extraordinary behaviour that was to remain a cause of opposition to him in certain quarters for the rest of his life.

Apart from his formal theological studies - at which, it seems, he excelled - he had his own personal programme of reading, greatly facilitated by his appointment as librarian in the seminary. This gave him the opportunity, which he himself claims he took, to become familiar with all the best books of spirituality available at that time; most especially those dealing with the Blessed Virgin and devotion to her. We still possess some of his notebooks into which he copied many passages that appealed to him on this topic, as well as notes for sermons - he was already preparing for a life of preaching as a missionary.

Ordination

After seven or eight years in Paris, Louis Marie was ordained priest there on 5th June 1700, Pentecost Sunday; and a few days later he said his first Mass in the parish church of Saint-Sulpice, in what is today the Lady Chapel. His friend, Jean-Baptiste Blain, who had followed him to Paris to study for the priesthood, tells us that "he was like an angel at the altar" on this occasion.

For a few months he seems to have hesitated as to his next move. There is evidence that some of the Sulpicians wanted him to stay on the staff at the seminary. But this was not to the taste of Louis Marie, who had thoughts of going as a foreign missionary to Canada, but was firmly dissuaded from this. Eventually, around September 1700, he went to Nantes to join the community of Saint-Clément, founded by a saintly priest, Fr René Levesque. He was hoping that this would be the start of his life as a preacher of missions.

Early Hopes and Frustrations

As is clear from a letter Louis Marie wrote on 6th December 1700 to his spiritual director, Fr Leschassier, he found that the situation at Saint-Clément gave him little hope of getting started on his preferred apostolate, "mission work, and especially teaching catechism to the poor". We sense his frustration as he dreams of going "in a humble and simple way to teach catechism to the poor in country places and to arouse in sinners a devotion to our Blessed Lady." He sees the needs of the Church, and in view of these proclaims that he "cannot help pleading continually for a small and poor band of good priests to do this work under the banner and protection of the Blessed Virgin" - the first indication of his desire, developed urgently later on, to found what was to become the Company of Mary.

In April of the following year, Louis Marie went to the Abbey of Fontevrault, near Saumur, where his sister, Sylvie, was about to make her religious profession. There he met Madame de Montespan, the former mistress of the king, Louis XIV, who, after her banishment from the court of Versailles, had made her peace with God and the Church. This was not the first time Louis Marie had met her, and she showed a great interest in his desires.

On her advice, he now made a journey to Poitiers to seek
an audience with the bishop there, in the hope of getting
started on the work of missions. But before he could meet
with the bishop, circumstances led to his being requested
for the post of chaplain to the General Hospital in that city.
Although this would certainly give him the opportunity to
serve his beloved poor, he did not see this as the answer to
his personal desires. However, after several more months,
during which he did have an opportunity to give some
missions in the Diocese of Nantes, which delighted him, he
finally agreed to the request of the Bishop of Poitiers and
took up the post of chaplain in Poitiers at the beginning of
November 1701.

Chaplain in Poitiers

The General Hospital was in a very sad state, both
spiritually and materially, according to Louis Marie, who
immediately set about trying to bring some reforms to the
place. He met with great opposition, however, especially
from the members of the Board of Directors, who seem to
have been enjoying something of a sinecure. He struggled
on, however, and was somewhat consoled by encountering
a young woman, Marie-Louise Trichet, whose direction he
undertook, and who shared with him his love for the poor
and was eventually to become the first of his congregation
known as the Daughters of Wisdom. The disputes with
the Board of Directors continued, and eventually, after

The General Hospital in Poitiers (1701-1705).

some seventeen months of frustrating confrontations with those in charge, Louis Marie left the Hospital and in April 1703 left for Paris, where he found, for the most part, only rejection by his former teachers at Saint-Sulpice, and desertion by the majority of his friends and acquaintances. This seems to have been the result of reports emanating, perhaps maliciously, from the Hospital in Poitiers.

Despite his desertion by so many of his former friends in Paris, he retained a few, notably the Jesuits who had their novitiate near his own poor lodging, and his former schoolmate, Claude Poullart des Places, who had just started a community that would become the Congregation of the Holy Spirit, and a seminary for the training of poor students for the priesthood. To the first students there Louis Marie gave a retreat, which seems to have formed the basis for his earliest writing, *The Love of Eternal Wisdom*. After eleven months or so of miserable living conditions in Paris, he was invited by the Bishop of Poitiers, at the request of the poor inmates of the General Hospital in Poitiers, to return there, this time as Director as well as chaplain. It might have been expected that this position would give him more control over conditions in the hospital; but in fact opposition to his proposed reforms on the part of the governors and administrators continued unabated, and after another year or so, Louis Marie finally withdrew, with the approval of the bishop, to take up what had always been his preferred form of apostolate, the giving of parish missions.

From about June 1705 to about March 1706, he gave missions in various parishes of the city of Poitiers, beginning with one in a poor section of the parish of Sainte-Radegonde in the suburb of Montbernage. There he established many of the characteristic traits of his later missions: his choice of the poorest parts of a parish to concentrate his personal efforts on; the restoration or refurbishment of the places of worship; the use of visual aids and of hymns set to popular tunes to help the evangelisation of the simple, unlettered people; an insistence on the Rosary as a means of perseverance in the good resolutions resulting from the mission. All of these endeared him to the simple shopkeepers, housewives and working men of the town, but, for some reason, aroused the opposition of many of the bourgeoisie and a few of the clergy. Perhaps it was just that his choice of the poorer people was seen as an insult to the middle classes. Whatever the reason, some of the clergy managed to turn the bishop against him, and he was ultimately ordered to leave the Diocese of Poitiers.

Pilgrimage to Rome

This was a severe blow to his self-confidence, and seems to have caused him to question whether his choice of parish missions was indeed inspired by the Holy Spirit. He saw no other way of resolving his dilemma than going to the very top: he would make a pilgrimage to Rome to consult the Vicar of Christ himself, Pope Clement XI, as to where his vocation lay. So, leaving behind in Poitiers the young Marie-Louise Trichet - who had by this time gone to live in the General Hospital while waiting to see how her own vocation would be fulfilled - and a young man, Mathurin Rangeard, who had been invited by Louis Marie to join him in his work, and who was to remain faithful to this for the rest of his life, he set out on foot to make the long journey to Rome. With a small detour to visit the famous shrine of the Holy House of Nazareth in Loreto, he arrived in Rome towards the end of May, and was received in audience by the Pope on 6th June 1706.

He poured out his heart to the Holy Father, telling him of his doubts as well as his ways of doing things, and offering his services to the foreign missions in India or further afield. But Pope Clement told him: "You have a wide enough field of action in France for the exercise of your zeal, my son. Do not go elsewhere, and work always in perfect submission to the bishops of those dioceses to which you will be called. In this way God will bless your labours." And with that, the Pope bestowed on him the title of 'Apostolic Missionary'. For Louis Marie, the way was now perfectly clear - God had spoken in the person of his Vicar. So he set off home with a mandate to continue the work of parish missions he had been doing in Poitiers. Meeting Mathurin Rangeard just outside Poitiers, he continued on his way towards Brittany, where he seems to have had some idea of joining M Jean Leuduger, the great missionary whose work had inspired him during his days at the Jesuit College in Rennes.

Missionary work continues

After making a retreat at Mont-St-Michel, he passed through Rennes, and possibly his native town of Montfort, to arrive towards the end of the year in Dinan, where he joined the team of missionaries who were giving a general mission in the town; and either then or a few weeks later he finally met M Leuduger and joined his team of missionaries. For the next few months, he worked with this team giving missions in various places in the dioceses of Saint-Brieuc and Saint-Malo, including, it would seem, in his own native town, Montfort. During these missions, he usually opted to take on the poorest areas of the parishes, and to carry out his favourite occupation of teaching the catechism. But he also made something of a name for himself as a restorer of ancient chapels, and as one who could bring about reconciliations between warring parishioners. Perhaps this engendered a certain jealousy in the other members of the mission team, or perhaps his way of doing things was just seen as very different from theirs. Whatever the reason, after a few months of very hard work, and following a rather futile argument concerning the collecting of alms, M Leuduger dispensed with his services during the summer of 1707.

This period of giving missions with the mission team led by M Leuduger, was certainly a valuable apprenticeship for Louis Marie, even if he had already begun to develop his own style in the missions. Among those personal and somewhat unusual elements that he would incorporate in all his future missions were two in particular: first of all the practice of relying entirely on the people of the parish where he was preaching for the needs of the missionaries, without taking any fixed stipend or making any prior arrangements for the financing of the mission - unlike the commonly used system at that time of 'funded' missions; and secondly his involvement of the lay-people as much as possible in various aspects of the mission, and particularly in caring for the needs of the poor during it.

Hermitage of Saint-Lazare

But for now, finding himself once again rather thwarted in his ambitions, he felt the need for a period of prayer and contemplation, and so he went to spend several months, perhaps even a year, in a hermitage just outside Montfort, called Saint-Lazare. There, with Mathurin Rangeard (by now known to everyone as Brother Mathurin) and another young man, Jean, who had joined him as a coadjutor brother like Mathurin, he formed the first community of what was later to become the Company of Mary. They prayed together, they fasted together, and together they renovated the chapel at Saint-Lazare and made of it a place to welcome the people of the surrounding area. If he had hoped to be left alone to contemplate, Louis Marie was soon thwarted in that too, as crowds began to gather to hear him speak of the love and mercy of God. First they had to leave the little chapel and gather the people in the open air to hear him preach, then he began to preach in the market-places and squares of the surrounding towns and villages. This did not go down well with some of the local clergy, who succeeded

Only known portrait of Louis Marie painted shortly after his death, preserved at Saint-Laurent-sur-Sèvre.

in having him banned from preaching except in the parish churches (and almost banned altogether), and that seemed to include even Saint-Lazare. It seemed, despite some very successful missions preached in the surrounding area, this was too much for Louis Marie, who decided to leave his native region and return to the Diocese of Nantes, where he had first attempted his mission apostolate during his stay in Saint-Clément.

Missions in the Diocese of Nantes

The Diocese of Nantes, to which Louis Marie returned about the middle of 1708, was to be the scene of some of his greatest missionary successes, but also that of his most painful reverse. He was fortunate to have a friend there in the person of one of the Vicars General, Fr Jean Barrin, who may indeed have been the one who invited him to return in this year. With Fr Barrin's encouragement, and sometimes his active intervention in parishes where the parish priest seemed reluctant to engage a missionary, Louis Marie began a series of missions that took him all over the diocese. He began in Saint-Similien in Nantes itself, then conducted missions in Vallet, La Renaudière, Landemont, La Chevrolière, Vertou and Saint-Fiacre. He was accompanied in many of these missions by a young priest, only recently ordained, Fr Pierre Ernaud des Bastières, who was to become one of his most faithful friends and collaborators, though he was not willing to commit himself to join the longed-for Company of Mary, and indeed found it hard sometimes to keep pace with the energy and even ruthlessness of Louis Marie's style.

Most of these missions were a great success and were heartily welcomed by the parish priests concerned. In a few, however, there was positive opposition on the part of the parish priest to the idea of a mission, and in those cases the authority of the Vicar General or the gentle reaction of Louis Marie himself had to be exerted to bring agreement - such was the case of La Chevrolière, for example. But by this time Louis Marie was so used to his missions being accompanied by difficulties and crosses that, when some particular parish presented no difficulty at all (as in the case of Vertou), he was quite disconcerted and suspicious. It was in Vertou that he told the astonished Fr des Bastières, when he realised that things were going very well, that they should probably leave, as such lack of difficulties could mean only the lack of success: "No cross: what a cross!"

Mission features

In the missions he gave in these years, we see also some of the features that became a regular part of his missions. For example (although this idea was not a completely new one, having been introduced by a famous missionary who went before him, Julien Maunoir), he had banners made in Nantes illustrating the mysteries of the Rosary and other Catholic doctrines, which he used as visual aids. He organised big processions through the towns and villages, during which the hymns he wrote himself would be sung - a very effective way of teaching the simple people the truths of the faith, and the processions themselves being a manifestation of the faith of the people. He often took advantage of the good will of the people during the time of the mission to have the churches cleaned and renovated, and especially, wherever possible, to have the custom of burying the dead in the church itself given up by the parishioners. Sometimes he would try to renovate a small shrine, particularly a Marian one, that had fallen into disuse. He would always end the mission by the solemn erection of a mission cross, which would remain as a reminder of the fruits of the mission. Occasionally (as later in La Rochelle) more than one cross would be erected in different parts of the region. And sometimes he would erect, not just a cross, but a spectacular Calvary. We shall see that this was his project in Pontchâteau, but later also in other dioceses he would introduce the same idea. He had already (in his own native town of Montfort) tried to erect such a Calvary, but in the end this was forbidden; he kept the statues he had commissioned for this for a later date.

A particular focal point of all his missions was a solemn renewal of the vows of Baptism. For this he would organise a special service which would often begin outside the church. The people would process into the church and make their way, one by one, to the baptismal font, where they would solemnly declare their intention to live up to their baptismal commitments and would bless themselves with the water in the font. They would then make their way to the altar or chapel of Our Lady, where they would make a special offering, asking her to aid them in their Christian lives. And finally, where possible they would sign, or make their mark on, if illiterate, a 'Contract of Covenant with God', by which they would promise, as though making a legally-binding contract, to remain faithful to their commitment to follow Jesus Christ for the rest of their lives. Part of the 'Covenant Contract' would state: "I give myself entirely to Jesus through the hands of Mary, to carry my cross after him all the days of my life." It was Louis Marie's belief, clearly stated in his book *True Devotion to the Blessed Virgin*, which he was to write later on, that genuine devotion to Our Blessed Lady was one of the principal means of developing a right relationship with Christ (or acquiring divine wisdom - the only true wisdom being Jesus Christ incarnate himself - as he had put it in *The Love of Eternal Wisdom*), and in all his missions he taught that the most perfect form of devotion to Mary was a total gift of oneself to Jesus through her hands - hence this statement in the 'Covenant Contract'.

In all his missions, St Louis Marie sought to give concrete expression to devotion to both Christ and his mother, Mary, through the establishment of the regular recitation of the Rosary. He requested, and obtained from the Master General of the Dominicans, the right to establish the Confraternity of the Rosary wherever he preached missions. This was to continue for the rest of his life.

Most, if not all, the missions he gave in Nantes diocese in 1708 were to the south of the great River Loire. In 1709, he turned his attention to those parts of the diocese to the north of the Loire, beginning with Campbon. Here he had the church renovated, as had become his usual practice, but in doing so, he inadvertently sowed the seed that would ultimately result in his greatest reverse: he painted over the coat-of-arms of the Duc de Coislin, the patron of the church in Campbon. As we shall see, it was probably this act that aroused the ire of some of the local nobility, with subsequent disastrous results.

The Calvary at Pontchâteau

Following the mission in Campbon he preached a mission in Crossac - where he had perhaps the most striking success in having the practice of burial in the church abandoned - and then, in mid-April, he arrived in Pontchâteau to begin the mission there. This was to be, in some ways, his greatest triumph, but also his greatest failure. He had been dreaming for some years of erecting a spectacular Calvary that would remind everyone of the sacrifice of their Saviour on the Cross. He had attempted to build such a Calvary in Montfort. Now, just outside Pontchâteau, on the raised 'Lande de la Madeleine' (Magdalene Heath), he thought he had found the ideal place. During the course of the mission he discussed his idea with the clergy and the people, and everyone was enthusiastic. So, at the end of the mission, towards the end of May, the local people began to construct the Calvary. It was to be much more than just a simple mission cross. An artificial mound had to be raised by taking earth from a moat surrounding the mound; and, not only were all the characters who had been present at the death of Jesus - his Mother, Mary Magdalene, St John, the two thieves and the soldiers - to be represented there, but surrounding the Calvary there were to be chapels and monuments representing all fifteen mysteries of the Rosary; in short a whole catechesis in visual form of the mysteries of the life of Christ and his Blessed Mother.

The force of his personality enabled Louis Marie on this occasion, perhaps more than at any other time, to inspire hundreds, even thousands of people to take part in this great enterprise. Fr des Bastières tells us that there would be as many as five hundred to six hundred people working on the construction of the Calvary at any one time, many of them not of peasant stock, but bourgeois and nobles as well. The fame of what was happening was so great that the story even spread, it is said, to England, from where some of the beleaguered Catholics of that country - the penal laws against Catholics following the English Reformation were still very much in force - came to lend a hand.

The work on the construction continued throughout the summer and autumn of 1709. In the meantime, Louis Marie and his faithful friend Fr des Bastières, along with Brother Mathurin, continued conducting missions in the surrounding areas: in the area known as the Grande Brière, and in Missillac. As 1709 gave way to 1710, the missions continued: in Herbignac and Camoël; then a mission in the parish of Saint-Donatien in Nantes itself, followed by one in Bouguenais, again south of the Loire. Between missions, and whenever he could find a short interval when he could get away, Louis Marie was back in Pontchâteau supervising the building of the Calvary. At last, all was finished, the date for the solemn blessing had been fixed (with the bishop's approval) for Sunday, 14th September 1710, the Feast of the Exaltation of the Holy Cross, and four eminent preachers had been persuaded to preach to what was expected to be a huge crowd. Thousands of people began to arrive for the inauguration. More than twenty thousand turned up, according to some reports, their number including Jean-Baptiste Grignion, Louis Marie's own father, and other members of his family.

Then, the night before the planned inauguration, came a completely unforeseen blow: word came from the Bishop of Nantes that the blessing of the Calvary was forbidden! No explanation was given, so Louis Marie immediately set out on foot to go to Nantes. Having walked all night he had an audience with the bishop, who informed him that the prohibition had come directly from the Royal Court at Versailles. Not only that, but the whole Calvary complex was to be demolished. It transpired that the agent of the Duc de Coislin, whose coat-of-arms Louis Marie had caused to be painted over in the church at Campbon, had set in train a rumour that what was being constructed in Pontchâteau was a possible fortress that could give refuge to invading English troops - France was then actively engaged in the

The Calvary of Pontchâteau, restored in the nineteenth century.

War of the Spanish Succession, against England and her allies in the Grand Alliance; Louis XIV's armies had already suffered major defeats by the Duke of Marlborough and Prince Eugene of Savoy at Ramillies, Oudenarde and Malplaquet, and the fear of invasion was rife. Ridiculous as the claim that Louis Marie's Calvary was in reality a fortress might be, those far from the actual situation chose to believe the rumours, and the Calvary was doomed.

Setbacks

This was certainly a most severe blow to all Louis Marie's hopes and dreams, but, as usual, he took the blow calmly, merely remarking that if God wished the Calvary to be saved, he would see to it, and then he went off to begin another mission in the nearby Saint-Molf. But there he was to suffer a second grievous blow - he received word that he was no longer allowed to preach in the Diocese of Nantes. No doubt the bishop had been severely shocked by the royal edict forbidding the Calvary, and discretion seemed to dictate to him that the perpetrator of such a threat to national security, Louis Marie, should be reined in. Again, Louis Marie took the blow with calmness and resignation. He went off to make a retreat in the house of the Jesuits in Nantes, where the director of the house was astonished by his equanimity in the face of what had happened.

Though his licence to preach had been revoked, Louis Marie was still able to minister in other ways to the people sent to him by God. For the next five or six months, from the end of September 1710 until Lent of 1711, he occupied himself with the poorest in the town of Nantes. He established a small hospital for incurable patients in the town, and in the early days of 1711, when the Loire flooded, cutting off a whole suburb of the town, he was able, at the risk of his own life, to bring the people of that suburb relief.

In the meantime, the demolition of the Calvary at Pontchâteau was begun, but, after a while, the local people showing extreme reluctance and resistance, it was abandoned, with just the various statues having been taken away, to be stored somewhere else for a possible future use. Over the next century and a half, a number of efforts were made to restore the Calvary, and finally, in 1821, it was re-constructed almost as Louis Marie had envisaged it, by the parish priest of Pontchâteau of that day, Abbé Gouray.

After several months, as the bishop showed no signs of lifting the prohibition of preaching inflicted on Louis Marie, he who had for so long seen the preaching of missions as his God-given vocation, backed up by the command of the Pope himself, decided at the beginning of Lent 1711 to take up invitations that had come to him from the Bishops of Luçon and La Rochelle to go to minister in their dioceses. And so he left Nantes to begin the final phase of his life, in which he finally found peace and tranquillity enough (though not without trials, some quite severe) to fully realise his missionary potential.

Last Years

He began with a mission in La Garnache in the Diocese of Luçon. He was due to give another in Saint-Hilaire, but, taken in by adverse rumours regarding Fr de Montfort, the parish priest there refused to let him start the mission. Perhaps this reverse was one of the reasons why Louis Marie did not give very many missions in the Diocese of Luçon, most of those in the next few years being in the Diocese of La Rochelle. There were, however, two or three in Luçon diocese, notably the Ile d'Yeu in Lent 1712, Salertaine in May of that year and Saint-Christophe-du-Ligneron in June. After being turned away by the parish priest of Saint-Hilaire, he went to the town of Luçon itself, where he was invited to preach in the cathedral before the bishop, Mgr de Lescure. This good bishop hailed from Albi in the South of France, the centre at the beginning of the thirteenth century of the Albigensian heresy; but Louis Marie did not know the bishop's history, and, as he was preaching on one of his favourite topics, the Rosary, and the marvels its recitation could work, he spoke long and feelingly about the conversion of so many Albigensian heretics by St Dominic through the recitation of the Rosary. When, afterwards, he was informed that what he had said could perhaps annoy the bishop, he hastened to see his Lordship, who in fact received him and what he had said very graciously. Then on 11th May he made his way to La Rochelle, where the bishop, Mgr Etienne de Champflour, was to prove a real friend to him in the next five years.

Missions in La Rochelle

Louis Marie was asked first of all to give a mission in L'Houmeau, near La Rochelle. Then he began a series of three missions in the town of La Rochelle itself, separate ones for the men, the women and the soldiers. For these missions he pulled out all the stops, incorporating all his usual stratagems for making the occasion memorable and fruitful. He ended the mission for the women with a big procession, an illustrated record of which has been left to us by a certain M Claude Masse, an army officer, on whom the whole had made a great impression. His description includes a statement that "Even the Protestants were struck by his presence." La Rochelle had a large number of Protestants, with whom Louis Marie preferred to remain on good terms, rather than to enter into controversy, as indeed did the bishop.

Further missions in the various country districts of the Diocese of La Rochelle followed the great missions of the town itself; then at the beginning of Lent 1712, Louis Marie, as noted above, returned to the Diocese of Luçon to give missions in the Ile d'Yeu, Salertaine and Saint-

Christophe-du-Ligneron. The mission in the Ile d'Yeu was particularly notable for the difficulty the missionaries had in getting there. As war was still raging between France and England, among others, the coastal waters around France, and particularly around La Rochelle and the various ports to the north of it, were infested at that time by English 'pirates', as the French saw them, from Guernsey. Sailors were reluctant to take the missionaries out to the Ile d'Yeu for fear of these, and in fact, when they did find one willing to risk his boat on such a journey, they were closely pursued by an English ship, and very nearly captured. It seemed almost a miracle that they were saved, as Louis Marie persuaded them to recite the Rosary to ward off the danger.

Then, in the summer, it was back to La Rochelle for more missions and retreats in the various towns and villages of the diocese. From then until his untimely death three years later, he criss-crossed the diocese, preaching, and making sometimes unexpected conversions, such as, for example, of a certain Madame Mailly, a Calvinist who had been living in England but on her return to France was passing through La Rochelle when she heard of the fame of Fr de Montfort, entered into conversation with him, and was convinced, probably more by his charitable reception of her than by his arguments, of the truth of the Catholic Church. This incident also affords us a glimpse of the evolution that had taken place in Louis Marie over the years, particularly during his time in La Rochelle diocese.

Where, in his earlier days, he would often have appeared somewhat gauche in the presence of cultured women, and when he was often perceived as being on the side of the poor and rather opposed to the better-off people, he now seemed to be much more relaxed in both female and bourgeois or wealthy company.

Writing *True Devotion to the Blessed Virgin*

Autumn, the time of the harvest, was not a good time for holding missions in the countryside, as all the people would be needed to help in the harvest. So in the autumn of 1712, for example, Louis Marie was able to spend some time in a little house just outside the walls of the city, in the district of Saint-Éloi, that had been given him and furnished by a good lady from the town. Here he created a sort of hermitage for himself, where he could retire from time to time to pray and contemplate - and to write. It is thought that it was here in Saint-Éloi in autumn 1712, that he wrote the manuscript of the book for which he is best known, *True Devotion to the Blessed Virgin*. In this book, as in *The Secret of Mary*, written perhaps somewhat earlier, he sets out his teaching on the Blessed Virgin, and proposes as the most perfect form of devotion to her - and the most effective in bringing souls to Jesus Christ - a total consecration of oneself to Jesus through the hands of Mary. He says in the book itself that this is the teaching he has already been giving in all his missions for many years. He also foretells that the manuscript will be lost for a considerable time, a prediction that was proved true, the manuscript being hidden during the troubled days of the French Revolution towards the end of the eighteenth century, and only rediscovered in 1842, when the book was first published.

More missions and recruitment efforts

The end of 1712 and the first half of 1713 saw many more missions in various places throughout the Diocese of La Rochelle: Thairé d'Aunis, Saint-Vivien, Esnandes, Courçon, Beugnon, Bressuire, Argenton-Château and La Séguinière. The latter had as its parish priest one of quite a few Irishmen who had fled persecution in Ireland and were exercising their priestly ministry in France at that time - a Fr Keating, whom St Louis Marie was pleased to call "a parish priest after my own heart". At the end of this series of missions, Louis Marie was clearly almost exhausted, and he received an invitation from the sisters of Mgr Beauveau, the Bishop of Nantes, to go and rest for a while at their château. But Louis, perhaps sensing that his time on earth would not last much longer, and becoming more concerned about the establishment of the "band of good priests" he had dreamt of for so long - the Company of Mary - decided instead to make a visit to Paris to try to recruit some young men to join him in his work at the Seminary of the Holy Spirit, founded several years earlier by his old friend, Claude Poullart des Places. Poullart had died by this time, but his successors were willing to honour a promise he had made back in 1704 to Louis Marie to supply him with priests for his planned Company of Mary. On this visit in 1713, Louis Marie did not succeed in engaging any of the students immediately, but the seed was sown, and in fact the first priest to join his new foundation two years later, Fr Adrien Vatel, was one of those who listened to his words of encouragement during this visit.

After spending several weeks in Paris, Louis Marie returned to La Rochelle to continue his work of conducting missions throughout the diocese. But his health was now beginning to suffer from the punishing schedule he imposed on himself, and, after a mission in Mauzé he had to be hospitalised for almost two months, and to undergo various operations. At one point it seemed he was close to death, but eventually he pulled through. And then there began an even more punishing schedule of missions, including one in the neighbouring Diocese of Saintes, a series that took him up to the end of May 1714.

In June he undertook another long journey, this time to Rouen to visit another old friend of his college and seminary days, Jean-Baptiste Blain, by then a canon in the Cathedral of Rouen. It seems he was hoping to persuade his old friend also to join him in his hoped-for new foundation. In this he was doomed to be disappointed, as Blain was not built of the same stern stuff as himself, and was nicely settled into a comfortable ecclesiastical career - not at all the material

Louis Marie was looking for. This journey to and from Rouen lasted from June to November, as he and Brother Nicholas (and another, Brother Jacques, whom they picked up in on the way) made their way in what might be seen as a leisurely fashion via Nantes, Rennes (where they stayed for almost two months), Avranches, Villedieu-les-Poëles and Saint-Lô, to finally reach Rouen in mid-September. In Avranches, where they arrived on 14th August, the eve of the great Feast of the Assumption of the Blessed Virgin, Louis Marie was hoping to say Mass in the cathedral on the morning of the Feast. The bishop, however, having heard, it seems, rumours of the extraordinary behaviour of this "priest from Montfort", refused him permission and more or less told him to get out of his diocese. This was the occasion for Louis Marie to use a horse, seemingly for the only time in his active life, to carry him to the nearest parish outside the Diocese of Avranches, Villedieu-les-Poëles, in time to celebrate the Mass of the Feast. There were other adventures along the way, but eventually, after a rather fruitless meeting with his old friend, he returned by way of Nantes to La Rochelle.

Jean-Baptiste Blain had found his friend, he tells us, "dramatically changed, exhausted and worn out by work and penance." Yet this did not stop him from launching into yet more work, with at least five missions in December 1714 and January 1715, and at least three more between April and June; and it was at this time, too, that he began, with Bishop de Champflour, to organise free, charitable schools for the boys and girls of La Rochelle. He decided that it was now time to bring the two young women he had left behind ten years earlier, in Poitiers - Marie-Louise Trichet and a certain Catherine Brunet - to La Rochelle to take charge of the school for girls; while that for the boys was to be entrusted to some young men known as the 'Brothers in short cassocks' - perhaps a forerunner of the Brothers of St Gabriel who were to develop out of the group of male followers Fr de Montfort was to leave behind him.

The Daughters of Wisdom come to La Rochelle

He decided it was time too for the two young women (Marie-Louise and Catherine) to make religious vows, and thus formally establish the Daughters of Wisdom. A few other young women were to join them in the next year or so. His longed-for male missionary band was still without any permanent priest members, however; but in February 1715, Fr Adrien Vatel, who had listened to Louis Marie in Paris two years earlier, made the decision to join him instead of making his way to the West Indies, where he had been hoping to go as a missionary. A few months later, probably about October, a second recruit arrived on the scene: Fr René Mulot, a seemingly unlikely recruit who, though still only thirty-two years old, had been forced by very poor health to retire from active priestly ministry. He had come to Louis Marie to seek a mission for his brother's parish of Saint-Pompain; but Louis refused unless Fr Mulot would join him in conducting the mission that was about to take place in Vouvant, promising him that, if he agreed to do so, Fr Mulot would have no further health problems. This subsequently was proved correct, and Fr René Mulot became the successor of St Louis Marie himself in what had at last come into being: the Company of Mary.

Last missions and death

After the mission in Vouvant, there were just three more to be given by the indomitable missionary: that in Saint-Pompain, followed by one in the neighbouring parish of Villiers-en-Plaine. Then, after a final pilgrimage to Our Lady's shrine in Saumur - a place he had visited many times before - he arrived in Saint-Laurent-sur-Sèvre on 1st April 1716 to preach the mission there. It was to be his last. He was already suffering from a fever when he insisted on greeting the bishop when he visited Saint-Laurent during the mission, and preaching before him. After this, he had to take to his bed, suffering from pleurisy. On 27th April, realising his end was near, he dictated his will to Fr Mulot, and died the following day, 28th April 1716, at about eight o'clock in the evening. So ended a life of total dedication to the mission entrusted to him by God, a life that had touched thousands of souls, and that was destined, through his writings, to touch perhaps millions more.

Villiers-en-Plaine church where Louis Marie preached his last mission before his death during the mission in Saint-Laurent-sur-Sèvre.

At his funeral the day after his death, a vast crowd gathered - as many as ten thousand people, according to some reports - and his tomb in the parish church of Saint-Laurent - though he would certainly not have wanted to be buried inside the church! - soon became a place of pilgrimage, with tales of healings and conversions quickly lending it fame. Jean-Baptiste Blain, his old school friend, then the Canon of Rouen, was one of those who made a pilgrimage to the tomb a few years later, and claimed to have himself been cured there of a malady which had been troubling him for several years.

Just a few years after the death of the missionary, a new tombstone was placed over his grave, with an epitaph thought to have been composed either by the Marquis de Magnanne, a friend whom he had influenced during a stay in Rennes many years before, or Fr Jean Barrin, his friend the Vicar General from Nantes. The epitaph reads (in English translation):

Traveller, What do you see?
A light quenched
A man consumed by the fire of Charity
Who became all things to all men
Louis Marie Grignion de Montfort
If you ask what was his life:
There was none more holy;
His penance: none more austere;
His zeal: none more ardent;
His devotion to Mary: none more like St Bernard.
A priest of Christ, he showed forth
Christ in his actions, and preached
Him everywhere in his words.
Indefatigable, he rested only in the grave.
Father of the poor,
Protector of orphans,
Reconciler of sinners.
His glorious death was the image of his life;
As he had lived, so he died.
Ripe for God he passed to heaven
April 28th 1716
Aged 43 years

The Legacy of a Saint

Three hundred years after his death, St Louis Marie de Montfort continues to exert his influence in the Church, both as a missionary (through his followers in the Montfortian congregations) and as a fervent champion of Our Blessed Lady, his 'good Mother'.

Parish missions may have gone out of fashion in many parts of the world, but, as Pope St John Paul II insisted, evangelisation remains very much an imperative for the Christian Church. Evangelisation requires a deep understanding of the Christian message, only to be obtained through prayer and reflection; love of the Lord; and dedication to passing on the message of the Gospel using whatever means are at hand. Those means might still be preaching, writing, witnessing, teaching; or, today, the means of mass communication: radio, television and film. By his own example of dedication to the mission entrusted to him - by God and the Pope - St Louis Marie de Montfort still inspires the members of the Company of Mary, the Daughters of Wisdom and the Brothers of St Gabriel, to proclaim the Gospel in all these ways, and constantly to seek for new ways. They are joined in this enterprise by many thousands of lay-associates on every continent, and in many countries.

Statue of St Louis Marie de Montfort in St Peter's Basilica, Rome.

Legacy

Through his writings, St Louis Marie de Montfort has influenced thousands of Christians all over the world to seek a deeper relationship with God, especially through devotion to Mary. His teaching on devotion to the Blessed Virgin, and especially what he calls the 'perfect' form of devotion to her (total consecration to Jesus through Mary), expressed in *True Devotion to the Blessed Virgin* and *The Secret of Mary*, remains an inspiration to hundreds of thousands of people, just as it inspired such great figures as Pope St John Paul II, Frank Duff, Venerable Mother Mary Potter, and so on. His book *The Admirable Secret of the Rosary* encapsulates the importance he always attached to this devotion, which both he and Pope St John Paul II insisted is not just a Marian prayer, but a truly Christo-centric one. He was so convinced of the power of the Rosary for sanctification that, if a parish abandoned its practice after he had encouraged it in one of his missions, he was known to refuse to return to that parish. This conviction is echoed in Pope St John Paul II's Apostolic Letter, *Rosarium Virginis Mariae*, of 16th October 2002, in which the Holy Father cites St Louis Marie's book on the Rosary.

A somewhat neglected work by St Louis Marie, *The Love of Eternal Wisdom*, deserves deeper study, containing as it does the essential context of all his teaching regarding Mary - devotion to her being just one, even if the most powerful one, of several means to acquiring knowledge of and relationship with Christ. Another means that he mentions here is what he calls 'universal mortification', a theme that he takes up in another small book that he addressed to an association called 'Friends of the Cross'. *The Letter to the Friends of the Cross* explains the place of suffering and penance (the cross) in the life of the Christian, reflecting on the words of Jesus: "Anyone who wants to be a follower of mine, let his deny himself, take up his cross, and come after me."

Sound teaching on the love of God for each one of us, genuine devotion to the Blessed Virgin, the efficacy of meditation on the Rosary, and the importance for Christians of embracing the Cross of Christ: such is the written legacy of this great saint. May he long continue to inspire Christians of all ages and conditions, to be faithful witnesses to the Gospel.

The Montfortian Congregations

The Company of Mary (Montfort Missionaries)

Websites:
http://www.montfort.org.uk
http://www.montfort.org

UK Address:
V. Rev. Father Provincial, SMM
27 St Gabriel's Road
Cricklewood
London NW2 4DS

The Daughters of Wisdom

Websites:
http://www.daughtersofwisdom.org.uk
http://fdlsagesse.org

UK Address:
Rev. Mother Provincial, FDLS
Wisdom House
Romsey
Hants SO51 8EL

The Brothers of St Gabriel

Website:
http://www.stgabrielinst.org

Our Lady, Untier of Knots
Story of a Marian Devotion

Miguel Cuartero Samperi

During his studies in Germany, Pope Francis encountered a local devotion centred on an image of Our Lady in the Church of St Peter in Augsburg. Many had come to pray with seemingly irresolvable family and marriage problems and had been helped. On his return to Argentina he set about spreading this devotion and its novena. This booklet gives a brief history of the devotion and the main prayers to Our Lady Untier of Knots.

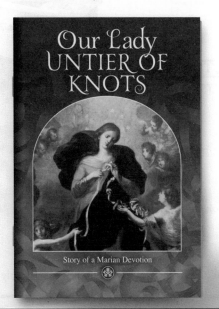

D769   ISBN 978 1 86082 901 7